# FRENCH for FUN

**Anna Nyburg**

*Illustrations by Richard Northcott*

**HARRAP**
London  Paris

First published in Great Britain 1990
by HARRAP BOOKS LTD
Chelsea House, 26 Market Square,
Bromley, Kent BR1 1NA

© Harrap Books Limited 1990

All rights reserved. With the exception
of the pages mentioned below, no part
of this publication may be reproduced in
any form or by any means without prior
permission of Harrap Books Limited.
The unnumbered central pages between
pages 10 and 11 may be photocopied
solely for use by the group or institution
for which the publication has been
purchased.

ISBN 0 245-60137-6

The accompanying cassette was recorded
at The Speech Recording Studio, London,
with Yves Aubert and Anne Engel.
The music is by John Kelham and
Roger Philbrick. The singer is Karine Blanco.

Printed in Great Britain
by the Hollen Street Press, Slough

# How to use *French for Fun*

You do not actually need to know any French to use *French for Fun* with your child. If you do it will help and if you don't, you are bound to learn some along the way!

The explanations and instructions in this book correspond to specific activities on the cassette. You should be ready to demonstrate the required actions and gestures, without giving too many explanations. "Watch me!" should really be sufficient. Avoid translating into English if you can. The children are bound to use their own language to interpret your actions or the French phrases they hear. Try to do no more than nod or shake your head, as in a game of charades. It will certainly all be easier for you if you can listen to each section before trying it out with the children.

These activities are even more fun if several people take part. Each child should eventually have a turn, not just at listening and responding, but at actually speaking as well. It is essential to speak for learning to take place and what is said must be close enough to the French pronunciation on the tape for you (and any others taking part) to understand and act on. If not, wind back the cassette so that you can hear the words again and encourage the child to copy a few times.

Be careful not to let the tape run on to the next section before the language of one activity has been assimilated through practice without the cassette. You'll hear the jingle **à vous maintenant** - *your turn now* - at those points where it's important to turn off the tape recorder and let the children have a go themselves.

The cassette recording has been structured to maintain children's interest and help you get the most out of *French for Fun*. Side 1 is for absolute beginners. It presents a sequence of basic activities, introducing phrases and vocabulary from scratch. Side 2 generally builds on Side 1. It goes back to many of the activities from Side 1, but introduces additional vocabulary. It also gives children the opportunity to show what they remember from earlier sessions, giving them that sense of achievement which is so important in the early stages of language learning. The table on page 1 shows you how these extension activities lead on from the basic activities, and where they are dealt with in this book.

The optimum time spent on *French for Fun* in any one session depends on the concentration and responsiveness of the child. A quarter to half an hour is probably plenty for most children.

Remember repetition is essential to language learning: try to include some of the activities from the previous session each time. Make language learning a positive experience. If your child doesn't respond well to one activity, try another. *French for Fun* is not intended as a comprehensive course but, as the title implies, an enjoyable way of helping your child realise that it is possible to learn to speak a language other than their own, with all the possibilities that that opens.

Many of these activities were developed at Honeywell Infants' and Junior School, Wandsworth. I would like to thank both the headmistresses and the Parent Teachers and Friends Association for their enthusiastic support, not forgetting the children who made the creation of *French for Fun* so much fun.

Anna Nyburg<br>London 1990

**SIDE ONE**
**Basic activities**

**SIDE TWO**
**Extension activities**

| page | | |
|---|---|---|
| 2 | *Bonjour!* | *Bonjour!* |
| 3-4 | Commands | *Jacques a dit* |
| 5 | SONG: *Meunier, ton moulin...* | |
| 6-7 | Counting | *Pincette* |
| 8 | *Chaud et froid* | |
| 8-9 | Colours | Colours (cont.) |
| 10-12 | Feelings and sensations | Feeling and sensations (cont.) |
| 13 | Number Bingo | |
| 13 | SONG: *Bateau* | |
| 14-15 | Touching objects | Touching objects (cont.) |
| 16 | What's your name? | How old are you? |
| 17 | | SONG: *Un, deux, trois...* |
| 18 | Weather | Weather (cont.) |
| 19-20 | What is it? | Word Bingo |
| 20-21 | Help! | |
| 22-23 | | *Une glace, s'il vous plaît* |
| 24 | | *Au revoir* |

You can work through the book listening either to Side 1 or to the slightly more advanced activities on Side 2. The illustrations will be relevant whether you are working with Side 1 or the corresponding extension activity on Side 2. However, it is important to be flexible. Try to create sessions to suit your children, moving around the book and going back to activities which they enjoyed last time.

The songs and one or two other items do not have a corresponding activity on the other side of the cassette.

un

# "BONJOUR"

When you hear the voice on the tape saying **bonjour** – *hello* – repeat it all together while shaking hands or waving at each other.

With younger children it is fun to make their soft toys pretend to say **bonjour**, always getting the child to answer. You can add your names...

**Bonjour Patrick!  Bonjour Anne!  Bonjour Hélène!  Bonjour Paul!**

When speaking to grown-ups it's polite to say **bonjour Monsieur** (to a man) and **bonjour Madame** (to a woman). These additional expressions are introduced at the beginning of Side 2.

*deux*

# COMMANDS

Now for some simple one-word commands. When you hear the first one – **assis!** – you should sit down smartly on the floor and get the children to do the same. Repeat the command while carrying out the action. This will help to associate the word correctly with the idea of sitting.

At **debout!**, the next one, you should jump to your feet. Then comes **couché!** – *lie down!* Keep responding to the orders, eventually stopping and seeing if your child can act on the command without copying you.

Once the children can do that without prompting – replay the tape if you still need more practice – it's their turn to give the command and you must sit down, stand up or lie down to order. Most children enjoy bossing others around for a change!

The pronunciation must be close enough to the original for you to identify it. If it doesn't sound good enough to you, play the tape back and ask the child to repeat the command.

| assis! | debout! | couché! |

When they are confident of those three you can move on to some more actions:

**sautez!** *jump up and down*
**courez!** *run about*
**tournez!** *turn around*

Now put all six actions together and again let the child have a turn at giving the orders.

'JACQUES A DIT...'

On Side 2 there is a reminder of these six one-word commands. Then a further dimension is added: the commands are used to play the French equivalent of *Simon Says* – **Jacques a dit...** (literally *Jacques said* ). Remember, if you don't hear **Jacques a dit,** you don't budge.

Again, once they are confident and can say **Jacques a dit** in a recognisable way, the child should have a turn at giving the orders – with and without **Jacques a dit**.

**A vous maintenant!**

It's worth remembering that quite small children will enjoy joining in with these simple actions, even though they won't be able to have a turn at giving orders.

If it is not possible to have more than one child involved in the activities, younger children might enjoy seeing a teddy or other toy doing all the actions. The more the merrier!'

**sautez!**   **courez!**   **tournez!**

# MEUNIER, TON MOULIN...

Now for a change, a song. It is often a good idea to listen to songs a few times, joining in the actions and perhaps a few words, then coming back to them on other occasions. It is surprising how songs seem to "learn themselves" in your head when you are not thinking about them.

Our first song has only a few words, but can be accompanied by vigorous windmill action. It is about a miller who lets his mill go too fast, and you can speed up the arm whirling when you get to the faster refrain.

> **Meunier, ton moulin, ton moulin, va trop vite**
> **Meunier, ton moulin, ton moulin, va trop fort**
> **Ton moulin, ton moulin va trop vite**
> **Ton moulin, ton moulin, va trop fort**

**Va trop vite** and **va trop fort** mean pretty well the same thing. The song could translate as follows:

> *Miller, your windmill's going too fast...*
> *Miller, your windmill's going too quickly...*

cinq 5

# COUNTING

While the tape plays the numbers, hold up the correct number of fingers. Ask the child to chant along with the tape, perhaps shouting, even if you're normally averse to too much noise.

When you are familiar with the sequence turn off the tape. You can hold up one finger, two fingers and so on, chorusing the numbers and gradually letting the children take over.

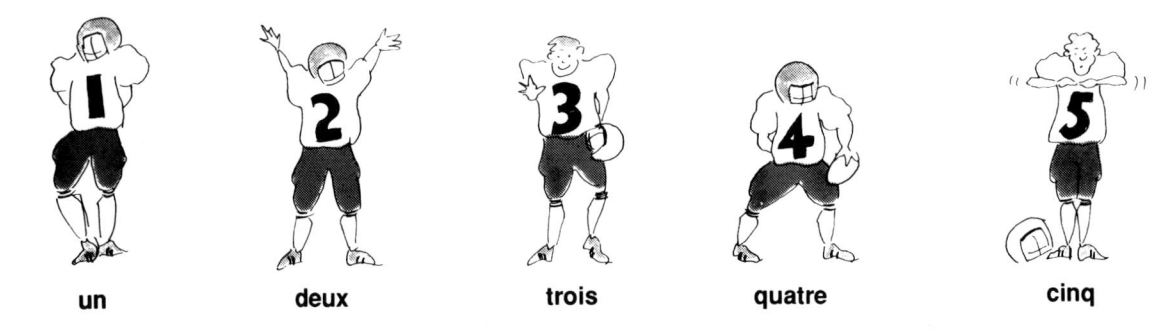

| **un** | **deux** | **trois** | **quatre** | **cinq** |

If you can, try holding up fingers at random to see if the child can give the French numbers out of sequence, though don't do too much of this at once. It is easier to become familiar with numbers in context – saying how old you are, asking for three ice creams, etc.

**trois glaces**

*six*

# "PINCETTE"

Of course there is another chance to practise these numbers on Side 2. Then you can try this counting game: "**pincette**".

Two people sit next to each other. One puts his/her hand on the other's knee and says **pain un**, which means "loaf one"... (well, it's only a nonsense game!). The other puts a hand on top and says **pain deux** – *loaf two*. The first person then puts their hand on top of the last hand and says **pain trois**. The other carries on the pattern with **pain quatre**. Now that all four hands are used, at **pain cinq** the first person must pull the bottom hand to the top of the pile. For **pain six** the second person does the same.

| six | sept | huit | neuf | dix |

Now for the point of the game: **pain sept** sounds the same as **pincette** which means *little pinch*. The person who says **pain sept** gives the other a little pinch. Ouch! or **aïe!** as it comes out in French...

See how long it takes for the child to work out that the person who puts their hand down first is the one to give the pinch!

sept

# 'CHAUD et FROID'

*très froid*

*froid*

Like hunt the thimble, this game consists of locating a hidden object by means of clues: "hot" for nearer and "cold" for further away from the object.

Before starting the French game, repeat **chaud** – *hot* – and **froid** – *cold* – a few times with the tape.

*chaud*

You can improve the game by adding **très** – *very*, e.g. **très froid** if someone is nowhere near the object.

The incentive can be increased by making the hidden object something small and edible. In fact occasional prizes of fruit, sweets and so on can help associate language learning with something pleasurable, although you may run into problems if you offer them automatically.

*très chaud*

# COLOURS

I find it is best not to introduce more than three colours at once to avoid confusion. Bring in the others in different sessions.

Use coloured paper squares to show the colours – the children can colour in their own – or point to the coloured balloons on the back of this book. On the tape you will hear **de quelle couleur c'est?** – *what colour is it?*

*huit*

**bleu** – point to blue balloon
**rouge** – point to red balloon
**vert** – point to green balloon

Do this a few times and ask the child to say it with you. Then play the words, now in a different order, and ask the child to point to the right colour.

Finally play the part of the tape which says **de quelle couleur c'est?** while you choose a colour to point to. You will probably know by now if the child is making the right response but you can of course check it against the coloured balloons.

If the child is still attentive, go on listening and learn three more colours in the same way:

**jaune**   *yellow*
**marron**  *brown*
**orange**  *orange*

Side 2 introduces three more colours: **noir** – *black*, **blanc** – *white* and **rose** – *pink*. We then continue with an activity to practise and consolidate all the nine colours we have looked at.

**Touchez quelque chose de...rouge** – *touch something...red* – though it might be blue, green, brown or whatever: that's the point of the game.

The cassette will give instructions and the children have to find and touch an object of the right colour. Perhaps you can "plant" a few around the room: an orange, a lemon, a black shoe, etc. Note how **de** becomes **d'** before the vowel in **quelque chose d'orange**.

*neuf* 9

Once they are happy doing the actions, again they can give the command: **touchez quelque chose de...** adding their choice of colour. Remember, if you can't understand it, it probably needs a little more practice with repetition first.

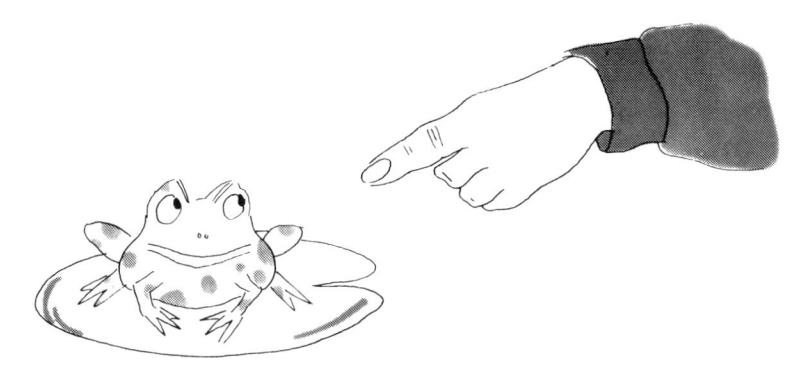

touchez quelque chose de vert

# FEELINGS and SENSATIONS

Here is where you really have to let yourself go and be ready to ham it up, exaggerating as much as you can to get the message across. The first time you play this part of the tape make the gestures and expressions appropriate to the statement. Let the children say in English what they think you're acting out, to make sure they are on the right track.

| | |
|---|---|
| **j'ai sommeil** | *I'm sleepy* |
| **j'ai faim** | *I'm hungry* – try rubbing your stomach and smacking your lips |
| **j'ai chaud** | *I'm hot* |
| **j'ai froid** | *I'm cold* |

For the last two, it's worth reminding them you have already played **Chaud et froid** so they might know those words.

Now let them do the actions along with you and the tape ("Can you show how you feel?") and say the words in French. You'll then hear the expressions in different order. See if the children can follow with the right actions.

These pull-out pages give you the bingo cards for *Number Bingo* and *Word Bingo*. The nine vocabulary cards will also be useful for your own bingo games.

These pages can be photocopied and stuck on card – and why not colour them in as well? To make your own set of snap cards, photocopy the nine vocabulary cards four times, then cut them out.

| | | |
|---|---|---|
| **un chat** | **une glace** | **une voiture** |
| **un gâteau** | **un chien** | **un bateau** |
| **une balle** | **une paille** | **le soleil** |

Card no.1 | Card no.2

Card no.3 | Card no.4

une

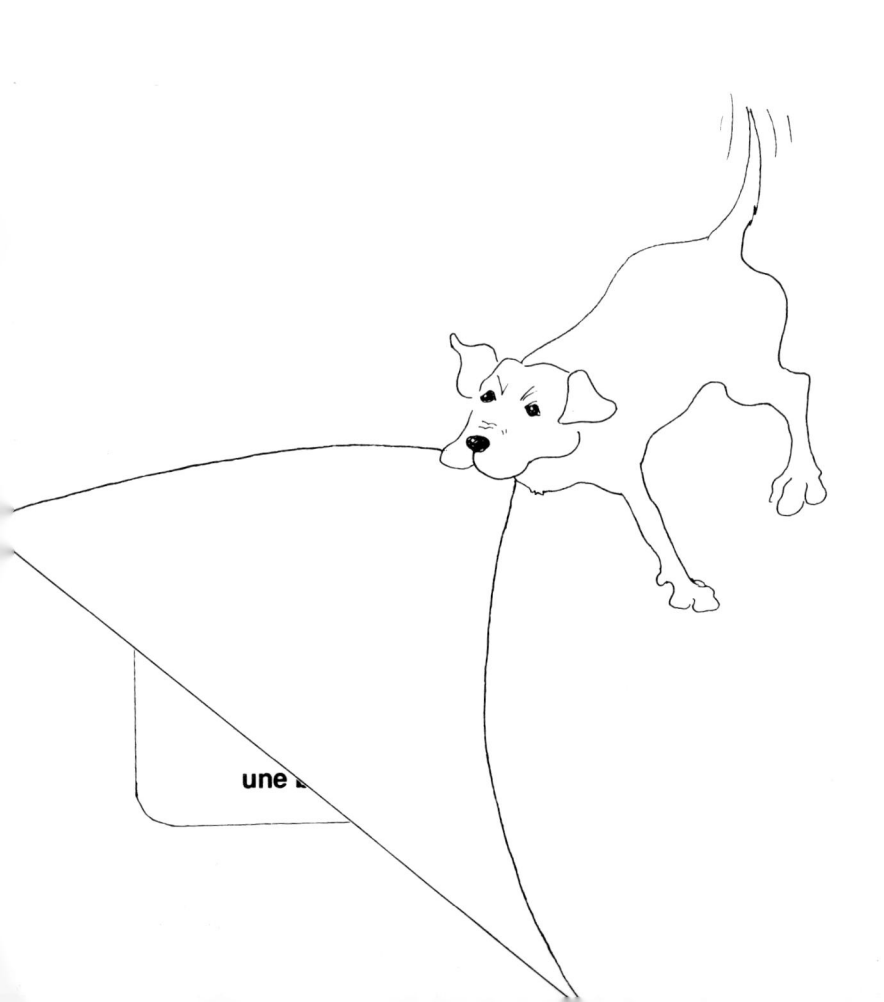

Finally, it is over to you to do the actions and see if they can say the phrase that corresponds to your mime. It might seem easier to you than the child, but remember, they haven't anything written to prompt them and the expressions do sound familiar to an untrained ear. If ever you find yourself getting frustrated or if they are getting tired of one section, it's time to give up immediately. Try to end on a positive note by offering one of the simpler activities: **Chaud et froid** seems to be popular.

| j'ai sommeil | j'ai faim | j'ai chaud | j'ai froid |

## A vous maintenant!

Side 2 brings in eight more feelings and sensations:

| | |
|---|---|
| **je suis triste** | *I'm sad* |
| **je suis content** | *I'm happy* - for a girl or woman **je suis contente** |
| **j'ai peur** | *I'm afraid* |
| **je suis en colère** | *I'm angry* |

**Je suis en colère** is always very popular, despite the length of the phrase, especially if you demonstrate tremendous fury, stamping your feet and shaking your fists!

| | |
|---|---|
| **j'en ai marre** | *I'm fed up* or *I'm tired of this* |
| **je suis malade** | *I'm ill* – maybe lie on the floor groaning horribly |
| **j'ai mal à la tête** | *I've got a headache* |
| **j'ai mal au ventre** | *I've got a tummy ache* |

You'll hear the phrases introduced in two groups of four, as shown above. With each group I recommend the same sequence of activities as on the Side 1 session:

1. The children listen to the cassette and you mime. They can say what the "feeling" is in English.
2. They mime to the cassette along with you, repeating the French.
3. The phrases come in different order. The children supply the appropriate mime. Help where you can.
4. **A vous maintenant!** - you do a mime and the children supply the French. With older groups you can probably pick individual children to mime for the others, once the French is thoroughly familiar.

| | | |
|---|---|---|
| je suis triste | je suis contente | j'ai peur |
| je suis en colère | j'en ai marre | je suis malade |
| j'ai mal à la tête | j'ai mal au ventre | à vous maintenant |

douze

# NUMBER BINGO

One round of this bingo game is recorded on the cassette (Side 1) but of course it will help learning if the children can go on to call out the numbers themselves. Use the bingo cards from the centre of the book. The only new word is **numéro** – *number*. Each number is repeated: **numéro un...un**.
Adults please note – the recording has been arranged so that card no. 1 is the winner.

# BATEAU

Like **Meunier**, this is a traditional children's song which has come down to us in many versions. You need to be in pairs, sitting facing each other with your legs stretched out in front of you. When the song starts join hands and rock backwards and forwards in time to the music, like the boat in the song.

**Bateau sur l'eau
La rivière, la rivière
Bateau sur l'eau
La rivière mène à Bordeaux**

Boat on the water
The river, the river
Boat on the water
The river goes to Bordeaux.

*treize* 13

# TOUCHING OBJECTS

We have already had some practice in giving and receiving commands, so the **-ez** ending of the imperative may be familiar: **touchez** – *touch*. If you are playing with one child, use the singular form, **touche**.

On Side 1 the object is to establish the words for *door*, *wall* and for certain parts of the body. Demonstrate the action along with the tape and, if possible, get the child to repeat the command.

| | |
|---|---|
| **touchez la porte** | *touch the door* |
| **touchez le mur** | *touch the wall* |
| **touchez la tête** | *touch your head* |
| **touchez le pied** | *touch your foot* |
| **touchez le nez** | *touch your nose* |

For the last one you can make a funny noise while pinching your nose to help associate **le nez** with *nose*.

As with previous activities, first ask the child to carry out the actions, responding to the command. It will help learning if they say the name of what they are touching as they do so, e.g. **la porte**. Then it is their turn to ask you to touch the objects. **A vous!**

*touchez la porte*

*touchez le mur*

*touchez la tête*

*touchez le pied*

*touchez le nez*

*quartorze*

Side 2 will give you this activity in a more varied and potentially more boisterous form. Use the same learning sequence: first they listen and follow the orders, then they give the orders.

A few further elements that should already be familiar are now brought into play...

| | |
|---|---|
| **touchez deux têtes** | *touch two heads* |
| **touchez deux pieds** | *touch two feet* |
| **touchez trois pieds** | *touch three feet* |
| **touchez trois nez** | *touch three noses* - a teddy or a doll might be needed here! |

At this point you will begin to hear **et** – *and* – which might need explaining. Try...

| | |
|---|---|
| **touchez la porte et le nez** | *touch the door and your nose* - not too difficult. |
| **touchez le mur et la tête** | *touch the wall and your head* |
| **touchez le nez et le pied** | *touch your nose and your foot* |
| **touchez deux nez et la tête** | *touch two noses and your head* |

Then how about these for a bit of fun:

| | |
|---|---|
| **touchez deux pieds...et la porte** | *touch two heads and the door* - this could be more of a challenge! |
| **touchez la tête et le mur** | *touch your head and the wall* |
| **touchez deux têtes et le pied...** | |

If you've understood the French you're probably in a heap on the floor by now, laughing!

quinze 15

# WHAT'S YOUR NAME?...

**comment tu t'appelles?**

If your children go on holiday to France and find some potential playmates it's good at least to be able to establish names and ages. This means both understanding and responding to the questions and being able to ask the questions themselves. Very often in a foreign country you're in a situation where you have to ask questions and language learners shouldn't be fobbed off with learning only to give answers.

*What's your name?* is **comment tu t'appelles?** (It could also be **comment t'appelles-tu?** but it's best not to confuse matters and to learn just one version.) Obviously a one-word answer is quite acceptable, but to say *my name is* or *I'm called* you say **je m'appelle**, which you can ask each child to say in turn.

**je m'appelle Ted**

Once again it is good to have plenty of material to practise on. If there are not several of you working together, rope in some toys which have names. Go round asking the toys and the child can answer for them. Then exchange roles: it is the child's turn to interview you and the toys.

**quel âge as-tu?**

The Side 2 session looks back over these useful phrases. Then you can go on to ask and tell ages:

> **quel âge as-tu?** – *how old are you?*
> **j'ai six ans** – *I'm six* (literally "I have six years")

Note that two French children talking to each other would automatically use the informal **tu** to say *you*.

**j'ai trois ans**

Numbers up to ten are on pages six and seven.

...HOW OLD ARE YOU?

16  *seize*

# UN, DEUX, TROIS...

If you are listening to Side 2, at this point you will come to a traditional French song. It practises counting up to 10 and adds on the next two numbers: **onze** – *eleven* and **douze** – *twelve*. Listen to the cassette for the pronunciation.

A few other new words are introduced as well. It might be easier to learn the song if you attempt it line by line. Use the pictures rather than the translation to fix words like **panier** and **cerises**.

**Un, deux, trois, nous irons aux bois**

**Quatre, cinq, six, cueillir des cerises**

**Sept, huit, neuf, dans mon panier neuf**

**Dix, onze, douze, elles seront toutes rouges.**

*One, two, three, we're going to the woods*
*Four, five, six, to pick cherries*

*Seven, eight, nine, in my new basket*
*Ten, eleven, twelve, they will be all red*

*dix-sept* 17

# WEATHER

For this it is fun – and a boost to learning – to have some props: an umbrella, a scarf or woolly hat, a pair of sunglasses. For **il fait chaud** *(it's hot)* you can fan yourself in an exaggerated fashion.

**quel temps fait-il?**

Start off by acting out the weather as you hear it on the cassette.

| | |
|---|---|
| **il pleut** | *it's raining* |
| **il fait froid** | *it's cold* |
| **il fait chaud** | *it's hot* |
| **il y a du soleil** | *it's sunny* |

**il pleut**

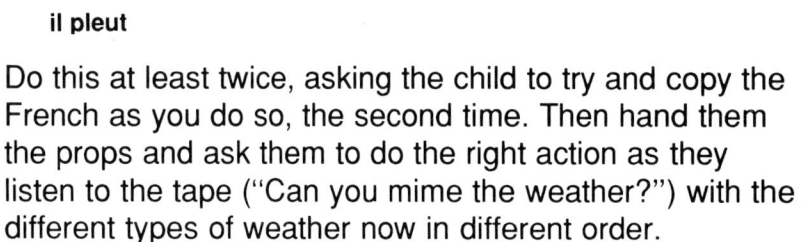

Do this at least twice, asking the child to try and copy the French as you do so, the second time. Then hand them the props and ask them to do the right action as they listen to the tape ("Can you mime the weather?") with the different types of weather now in different order.

**il fait froid**

Finally it is their turn to dictate to you: they hand you back the props and you do the actions.

### A vous maintenant!

On Side 2 you will hear how to ask what the weather's like in French: **quel temps fait-il?**. After a revision of the expressions given above, two more weather phrases are added:

**il fait chaud**

| | |
|---|---|
| **il y a du vent** | *it's windy* |
| **il neige** | *it's snowing* |

**il y a du soleil**

18 *dix-huit*

**il y a du vent**

The mime game mixes all six phrases. Follow through the same sequence of activities as before and finish with the children using French to dictate the actions.

**il neige**

# WHAT IS IT?

**Qu'est-ce que c'est?**...what is it?
For this you need to look at the pictures in order.

| un chat | une voiture | une glace | un gâteau | la mer |

| un bateau | une paille | un chien | une balle | le soleil |

Ask the child to say **Qu'est-ce que c'est?** and point in turn to the pictures. See if they can repeat the words. Try it again once or twice. Then it's your turn to point and see how many things they can manage.

*dix-neuf* 19

# WORD BINGO

Side 2 now gives you a second bingo game (**loto** in French) to consolidate the vocabulary learnt in the *What is it?* section. One "round" is recorded on the cassette but why not create your own game, using the vocabulary cards from the centre of the book.

This time shout **ça y est!** when you have a full card. The expression means more or less *there it is!* or *that's it!* and children very often use it when they hit the target or reach the winning square. You'll hear it on the cassette.

Adults please note — the recording has been arranged so that card no. 2 is the winner.

# HE-ELP!

The last activity on Side 1 of your cassette will appeal to more boisterous children. Just ask them to copy the tape while you act out some dramatic situations.

You'll hear three common French exclamations each structured in the same way: a noun preceded by the word **au**. **Au**, which usually means *to the*, is untranslatable in this context. It is a device French uses to draw attention to something.

**Au secours!** means *help!* Try wrapping your foot under a chair and waving for assistance. Or use your own hand to make it look as if you're being strangled!

**AU SECOURS!**

**Au voleur!** – *stop thief!* – could be more of a challenge if there is only one of you with one child. You really need someone to steal something from you (your shoe? a casually draped handbag?) so that you can pursue them shouting **au voleur!**

**AU VOLEUR!**

**Au feu!** – *Fire!* Here you could be a fireman trying to extinguish a fire with a hose.

They do the actions to the taped instructions. Then they can have fun pretending to be on fire, in difficulties or to have been robbed, shouting out appropriately. You can resort to violence if necessary by tickling them until they shout **au secours!**

**AU FEU!**

vingt et un 21

# 'une glace, s'il vous plaît'

You'll probably find by now that children will enjoy using their new language in what feels like a real-life situation. This little role-play activity is also a good preparation for life on the beach in France. Try it with props for extra realism.

We'll learn how to ask for an ice-cream—vanilla or chocolate—or a **crêpe**, a pancake which is usually cooked there and then and served in a piece of paper. First indicate the objects along with the tape and ask the child to repeat them at least twice:

une glace vanille

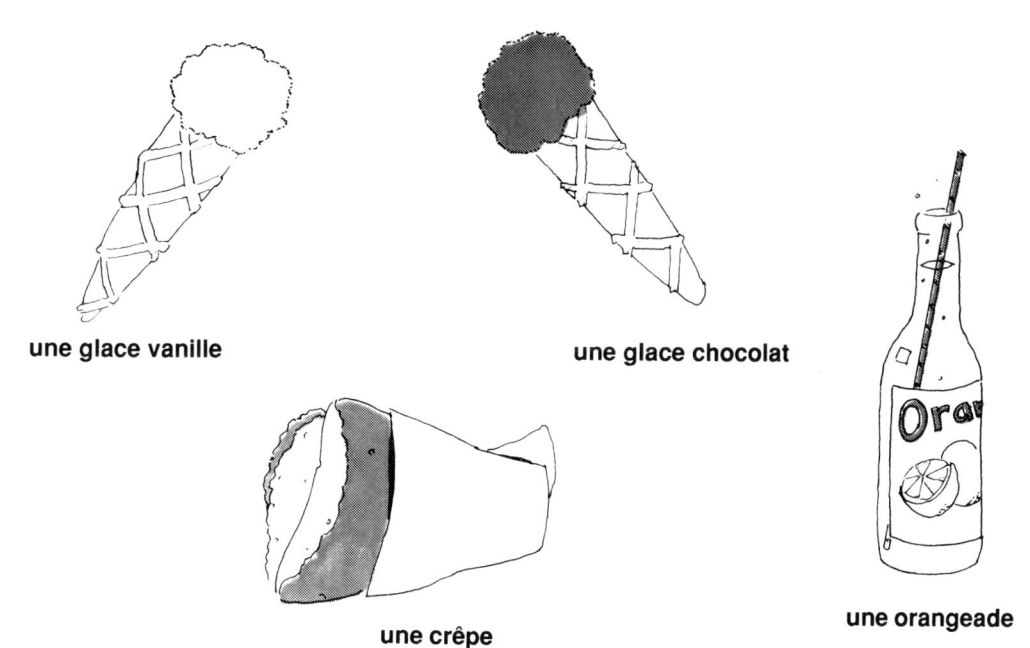

une glace chocolat

une crêpe

une orangeade

Then:
**s'il vous plaît** – *please* (or **s'il te plaît** when talking to a child)
**merci** - *thank you*

And to talk about prices:　　**un franc**
　　　　　　　　　　　　　　　**deux francs**
　　　　　　　　　　　　　　　**cinq francs**

Now listen to the dialogue:

| | |
|---|---|
| Child | **Bonjour Monsieur.** |
| Ice-cream man | **Bonjour. Qu'est-ce que tu veux?** |
| Child | **Une glace, s'il vous plaît** |
| Ice-cream man | **Vanille ou chocolat?** |
| Child | **Chocolat s'il vous plaît** |
| Ice-cream man | **Voilà. Cinq francs s'il te plaît.** |
| Child | **Merci** |

Listen a few times, asking the child to repeat the child's role. Then let them loose on the dialogue with gaps. Of course they can ask for a pancake or a drink instead in the second dialogue, which omits the **vanille ou chocolat?** choice, and asks for **trois francs** instead of **cinq francs**. Some free practising without the tape is also a good idea!

*vingt-trois* 23

*'AU REVOIR'*

At the end of Side 2 you will hear people saying *goodbye*: **au revoir**.
Again repeat it all together, wave and shake hands. Bring in the soft toys if there is only one child.

Like **bonjour**, **au revoir** could be followed by someone's name or by **Monsieur** or **Madame**. If you want to say "goodbye everybody" to a group of people, say **au revoir tout le monde**.